STRAWBERRY & OTHER BERRY DISHES

IMP Limited

Contents

STRAWBERRIES & BERRIES FROM AROUND THE WORLD

Berries are incredibly versatile fruits, either raw or cooked, whole or puréed. Here are some simple recipe ideas using berries, plus a handy visual guide to the different types.

PRETTY DECORATIONS

Use fresh berries to give your cakes, puddings and desserts that professional finish. Here are some simple ideas.

- Dip whole strawberries or cherries with stalks into melted plain, milk or white chocolate. Leave to set on greaseproof paper then use to decorate cakes, meringues or ice cream sundaes.
- Frosted red or blackcurrants make a beautiful decoration for gateaux, soufflés and mousses. Dip small bunches of currants in lightly beaten egg white and then in caster sugar. Leave to set.
- Spoon raspberry, blackberry or strawberry purée onto serving plates and top with individual sponge puddings, meringues or cake slices. For a marbled effect, swirl different colour purées together using a cocktail stick.

DISSOLVING GELATINE

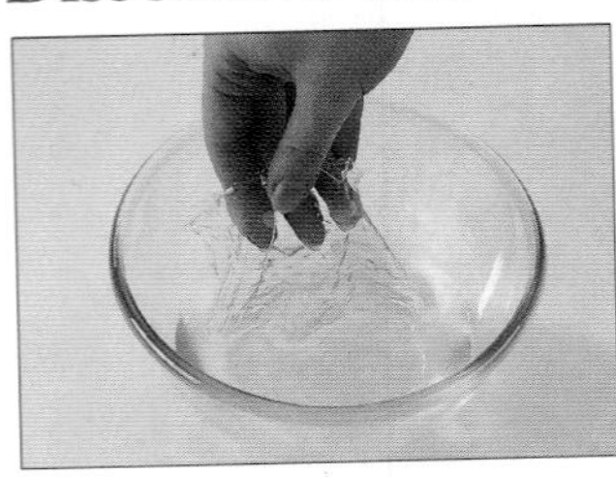

Soften leaf gelatine before use by soaking in cold water for 5 minutes. Squeeze out the excess water, then transfer to hot liquid to dissolve.

Sprinkle powdered gelatine over cold water and leave to stand until spongy (about 5 minutes). Stand the bowl over hot water until liquid is clear.

EASY BERRY RECIPES

- For a stylish summer dessert, try a fruit soup. Purée strawberries and add icing sugar to taste. Top up with sparkling wine or Champagne and serve.
- Flambéed fruit makes an impressive finale to a meal. Dip cherries in caster sugar to coat then fry in butter until the sugar forms a golden glaze. Add rum, brandy or kirsch and set alight with a long match. Cook over a low heat until the flames die down. Serve straight away.
- Use cranberries instead of raisins or currants in scones, teabreads and cake recipes.
- Add blackberries or cranberrie to a salad of mixed leaves, onion, tomato and blue cheese.
- Black or redcurrants make a tasty addition to gravy for your Sunday roast. Add red wine too for extra flavour.
- Crush over-ripe berries and soak in wine vinegar overnight. Use the fruity vinegar to liven u stews, casseroles, soups and pie fillings.

Berries At A Glance

Fresh cherries *(left)* are available for only a short time in summer and range from bright red to purply-black. When not in season, canned cherries can be used for cooking.

Blueberries *(above)* grow wild in the USA and are used in many favourite American puds, such as pies, pancakes and cheesecakes. They can also be eaten raw with a squeeze of lime or lemon juice.

Redcurrants *(right)* are usually cooked in jams, jellies and puddings to tone down their sharp flavour, or used as a pretty decoration for cakes and desserts.

Cranberries *(left)* are grown mainly in the USA. Too sour to eat raw, they are often used in pies or as cranberry sauce to serve with turkey.

Raspberries *(left)* are available fresh in summer months or frozen all year round. Sweet and tangy, they're eaten raw with cream or used in many hot and cold desserts.

Blackberries *(right)* are found wild in hedgerows in early autumn but are also grown commercially, mainly in the USA, then sold frozen or canned.

Strawberries *(right)* are grown all over Europe and North America and are eaten raw or cooked in many desserts. Avoid frozen strawberries as they can be very watery.

STRAWBERRY AND RHUBARB ROLL

GERMANY

This German version of the famous Austrian strudel uses shortcrust pastry for a less flaky result. Serve the roll warm to enjoy the lightly spiced fruit filling at its best.

INGREDIENTS
(Serves 4)

- 350g/12oz shortcrust pastry
- 1 egg
- icing sugar, for dusting

FOR THE FILLING

- 100g/4oz strawberries
- 225g/8oz rhubarb
- 4 tbsp caster sugar
- ½ tsp ground cinnamon
- ½ tsp ground nutmeg

INGREDIENTS TIP
Early rhubarb is forced into growth and has long, thin pale stems and a fresh flavour. Main-crop rhubarb is much coarser with a deep red skin and a sharp, tart flavour. Either can be used for this recipe. Never eat the rhubarb leaves as these are poisonous.

1 Preheat the oven to 200°C/400°F/Gas 6. For the filling, wash, hull and slice the strawberries. Wash and trim the rhubarb, then cut the stalks into thin slices.

2 Roll out the pastry on a lightly floured surface to a large oval or rectangle. Arrange the rhubarb and strawberries along the centre of the pastry, leaving a 1cm/½in border at each end.

3 Sprinkle the sugar, cinnamon and nutmeg over the fruit. Beat the egg in a bowl and brush over the pastry edges. Carefully fold over the sides of the pastry to enclose the filling. Brush the top of the roll with egg.

4 Transfer the roll to a baking sheet. Bake for 30 minutes, or until the pastry is golden. Dust the roll heavily with icing sugar, cut into slices and serve warm.

Step 1

Step 3

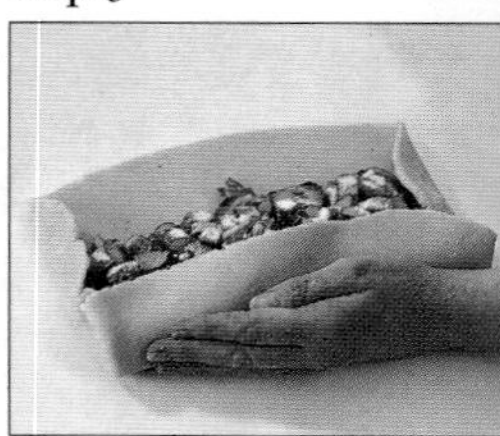

Step 3

Preparation: **20** Min Cooking: **30** Min
Per Serving: 507 kcal/2122 kJ;
6g protein; 27g fat; 65g carbohydrate

TYPICALLY GERMAN
Red fruits, particularly strawberries and raspberries, are popular in northern Germany. The countryside is dotted with farms where you can pick your own soft fruit for very reasonable prices. The berries are then used in delicious desserts like this one.

OOKING TIPS

Jse two large spatulas or fish slices to transfer the oll on and off the baking sheet • This recipe is deal for using up strawberries that may not be in heir best condition • For an extra hint of spice, ust the pastry with a little cinnamon or nutmeg nd roll in before adding the filling.

SERVING TIP

For a main course, roll a joint of pork in a mixture of crushed garlic, lemon rind and chopped herbs then roast until tender. Serve hot or cold with vegetables or a mixture of salads. Serve the berry roll hot for dessert with thick cream or custard.

SERVING TIP Serve this dessert after a main course of sausages or pork chops. Accompany them with hot sauerkraut for a traditional German taste, or with sautéed potatoes and roasted red onion wedges.

*B*LACKCURRANT MERINGUE SOUFFLE

GERMANY

A creamy blackcurrant mousse is topped with a layer of fluffy meringue in this elegant pudding. Perfect for entertaining, it makes a wonderful combination of colours and flavours.

INGREDIENTS

(Serves 6)

- 350g/12oz fresh blackcurrants
- 225g/8oz caster sugar
- 1 tbsp powdered gelatine
- 3 eggs, separated
- 284ml/10fl oz pot double cream

FOR THE TOPPING

- 3 egg whites
- 25g/1oz flaked almonds

INGREDIENTS TIP

Blackcurrants are in season in July and August. Their colour and intense flavour makes them a popular addition to many desserts, including pies, tarts and ice creams. To remove the berries from their stalks, hold them over a bowl and run a fork down the length of the stem.

1 Remove the blackcurrants from the stalks. Put the currants in a saucepan with 50g/2oz of sugar. Heat gently until the sugar dissolves and the blackcurrants are soft.

2 Meanwhile, put 3 tablespoons of water in a small bowl. Sprinkle over the gelatine and set aside until spongy. Set the bowl over a pan of gently simmering water until the gelatine is dissolved and transparent.

3 Purée the blackcurrants. Whisk together the 3 egg yolks and 75g/3oz of sugar until pale and thick. Add the currant purée and the gelatine mixture. Fold in the cream.

4 Whisk 3 egg whites until stiff peaks form. Fold into the purée mixture then pour into a 1.2 litre/2 pint soufflé dish. Cover with cling film and chill for 2 hours, or until set.

5 Preheat the oven to 230°C/450°F/Gas 8. For the topping, whisk the egg whites until stiff. Whisk in half the remaining sugar. Fold in the remaining sugar and spread over the blackcurrant mixture. Sprinkle with flaked almonds. Bake on the top shelf of the oven for 3–5 minutes, until the meringue is golden.

Step 3

Step 4

Step 5

reparation: **30** Min Chilling: **2** Hours
ooking: **5** Min
er Serving: 453 kcal/1894 kJ;
g protein; 28g fat; 45g carbohydrate

TYPICALLY GERMAN

The Palatinate region in the west of Germany is an important area for wine production. The best time to visit the picturesque local towns and villages is during, or just after, the grape harvest when there are lively festivals and the wine flows freely.

STRAWBERRY SOUFFLE

NORTHERN FRANCE

A mouth-watering combination of strawberry purée and sweet white chocolate makes up this light-as-air soufflé. Prepare it in advance and keep in the fridge ready to wow your guests.

INGREDIENTS

(Serves 4)

- 225g/8oz strawberries
- 175g/6oz white chocolate
- 40g/1½oz caster sugar
- 1 tbsp powdered gelatine
- 3 eggs, separated
- 284ml/10fl oz whipping cream
- 1 tsp vanilla essence
- extra strawberries and mint leaves, to decorate

INGREDIENTS TIP

White chocolate is made from cocoa butter, sugar and milk but doesn't contain cocoa solids like other chocolates. If you can find them, use white chocolate drops for this recipe to cut out the grating stage.

1 Cut a strip of greaseproof paper 5cm/2in higher than the top of a 900ml/1½ pint soufflé dish. Grease it well and wrap around the dish to make a collar. Secure with tape.

Step 1

2 Wash and hull the strawberries, then purée in a food processor or blender. Grate the chocolate. Put the purée into a pan with the sugar, gelatine and 2 tablespoons of water. Heat gently, stirring occasionally, until almost boiling. Remove from the heat and stir in the chocolate until melted.

Step 2

3 Beat the egg yolks in a large bowl and stir in the strawberry mixture until well blended. Leave to cool.

4 Whip the cream until soft peaks form and fold into the strawberry mixture, along with the vanilla essence. In a clean bowl, whisk the egg whites until stiff peaks form. Carefully fold into the soufflé mixture.

5 Pour the soufflé mixture into the dish and spread level. Chill for 3 hours, or until set. Remove the paper and serve decorated with halved strawberries and mint leaves.

Step 5

Preparation: **35** Min Cooking: **10** Min
Chilling: **3** Hours
Per Serving: 683 kcal/2837 kJ;
13g protein; 52g fat; 44g carbohydrate

TYPICALLY FRENCH

The gardens at the palace of Versailles are an amazing sight. With sculptures, fountains, a working farm and thousands of trees and flowers, they are a popular tourist spot. Both familiar and exotic crops flourish in the vegetable garden, from pumpkins to potatoes.

COOKING TIPS

o make individual soufflés, prepare four small amekin dishes with greaseproof paper collars as n Step 1. Divide the mixture between the dishes nd chill until ready to serve • Keep the chocolate n the fridge before using to make it easier to grate.

SERVING TIP

Savoury crêpes make an ideal main course before this fluffy soufflé. Fill the crêpes with any combination of grated cheese, ham, tomatoes, crispy bacon and sautéed mushrooms. Fold over the crêpes and top with a fried egg. Serve with French bread.

SERVING TIP Serve these pretty galettes with hot coffee flavoured with a generous measure of orange liqueur. Make sure you serve the desserts within an hour or two of making or the biscuits will turn soggy

*R*ASPBERRY AND ALMOND GALETTES

NORTHERN FRANCE

Crumbly almond shortcake biscuits are layered with a cream and fruit filling spiked with orange liqueur. These dainty treats are ideal as a stylish dessert or for a special afternoon tea.

INGREDIENTS

(Makes 6 galettes)

- 50g/2oz caster sugar
- 75g/3oz ground almonds
- 100g/4oz plain flour
- 75g/3oz unsalted butter, chilled
- 1 egg yolk

FOR THE FILLING

- 225g/8oz raspberries
- 1 tbsp icing sugar
- 1 tbsp orange liqueur
- 142ml/5fl oz pot double cream
- mint sprigs and icing sugar, to decorate

INGREDIENTS TIP

You can use other fruits in season instead of the raspberries, if you prefer. Try small strawberries or loganberries in summer, blackberries in autumn, or use chopped tropical fruit, such as kiwi fruit, in winter.

1 Preheat the oven to 180°C/350°F/Gas 4. Grease two baking sheets. Mix the caster sugar, almonds and flour in a bowl. Cut the butter into pieces and rub into the flour mixture until it resembles fine crumbs. Stir in the egg yolk and mix to form a soft dough.

Step 1

2 Knead the dough thoroughly then roll out on a lightly floured surface until 1cm/½in thick. Stamp out 12 rounds using a 7.5cm/3in fluted cutter. Arrange the rounds on the baking sheets and bake for 10 minutes, or until pale golden. Cool on a wire rack.

Step 2

3 For the filling, set aside about 18 raspberries for decoration and purée the rest in a blender or food processor, or mash them with a fork. Sift over the icing sugar and stir in, along with the liqueur.

4 Whip the cream until soft peaks form, then fold in the raspberry purée. Spoon the cream mixture onto six of the biscuit rounds. Sandwich together with remaining biscuits. Decorate with the remaining fruit and mint sprigs and dust with icing sugar.

Step 4

Preparation: **30** Min
Cooking: **10** Min, plus cooling
Per Galette: 406 kcal/1693 kJ;
6g protein; 30g fat; 29g carbohydrate

TYPICALLY NORMAN

Normandy on the north coast of France is an area of contrasts, from lively seaside resorts to wooded valleys and pine forests. The classic half-timbered houses around Caen and Pont l'Eveque give the area a picturesque charm that visitors find hard to resist.

MIXED BERRY BRULEE

NORTHERN FRANCE

INGREDIENTS

(Makes 8 desserts)

- 1 cinnamon stick
- 425ml/15fl oz single cream
- 175g/6oz fresh strawberries or raspberries
- 4 large egg yolks
- 50g/2oz caster sugar
- 1 tbsp cornflour
- ½ tsp vanilla essence

FOR THE TOPPING

- 4 tbsp caster or demerara sugar

INGREDIENTS TIP

Caster or demerara sugar is suitable for the topping. Demerara is a golden-brown sugar with large sparkling crystals. It is named after its place of origin in Guyana. It is traditionally used on cakes and bisçuits to give a crunchy topping. It is also good on cereal or in coffee.

A thin layer of crisp caramel covers the silky smooth custard in this favourite French dessert. This version has a fruity surprise of strawberries or raspberries at the bottom.

1 Put the cinnamon stick and cream in a saucepan. Heat gently until almost boiling. Set aside for 10–15 minutes, then remove the cinnamon stick. Meanwhile, hull and slice the strawberries, if using. Divide the fruit between 8 small ramekin dishes.

Step 1

2 In a mixing bowl, beat together the egg yolks, 50g/2oz caster sugar, the cornflour and vanilla essence with a wooden spoon until pale. Gradually pour in the cream through a fine sieve and beat until smooth.

Step 2

3 Return the mixture to the pan and heat gently, stirring constantly, until just below boiling point. Do not allow the mixture to boil. Pour the custard over the fruit in the dishes. Cover and chill in the fridge overnight to set.

4 Preheat the grill to high. Put the dishes in a roasting tin. Sprinkle a thin layer of caster or demerara sugar over each custard. Grill until the sugar just caramelizes and turns golden. Chill for 2 hours, or until the sugar layer is crisp.

Step 4

Preparation: **20** Min
Cooking: **10** Min, plus cooling
Chilling: **2** Hours, plus overnight
Per Dessert: 215 kcal/895 kJ;
3g protein; 13g fat; 23g carbohydrate

TYPICALLY PARISIAN

The Pompidou Centre is one of Paris's most talked-about attractions. Built in 1977, it houses the National Museum of Modern Art and a large library. Visitors flock to enjoy the lively atmosphere inside and out, where fun sculptures adorn the square.

OOKING TIPS

eaving the cream to cool with the cinnamon stick fuses it with a delicate cinnamon flavour • Make ire the custard mixture is smooth before returning the pan in Step 3. If lumps start to form, beat the ixture vigorously with a wooden spoon or balloon hisk until smooth.

SERVING TIP

Serve these chilled desserts after warming French onion soup. For a traditional finish, top each bowl of soup with a slice of French bread and sprinkle with grated Gruyère cheese. Put under a hot grill until the cheese melts. Serve straight away.

STRAWBERRY WINE MOUSSE

SWEDEN

INGREDIENTS

(Serves 6)

- 4 tsp powdered gelatine
- 450g/1lb fresh strawberries
- 3 eggs
- 50g/2oz caster sugar

FOR THE JELLY

- 2 tsp powdered gelatine
- 150ml/¼ pint red wine
- 2 tbsp icing sugar

INGREDIENTS TIP

If you don't want to use wine for the jelly, try red grape juice instead.

This double-layered delight comprises a light and luscious strawberry mousse underneath a luxurious layer of red wine jelly. Serve with crisp wafers for a crunchy contrast.

1 Sprinkle the 4 teaspoons of gelatine over 90ml/3fl oz of water and leave until spongy. Set over a pan of simmering water until the gelatine dissolves, stirring regularly. Leave to cool for 10 minutes.

2 Meanwhile, hull and purée the strawberries. Separate the eggs. Whisk the yolks and caster sugar until pale and thick. Stir in the puréed berries and the gelatine mixture until well mixed.

3 Whisk the egg whites until stiff peaks form. Carefully fold into the strawberry mixture. Spoon the mixture into serving dishes. Cover with non-PVC cling film and chill for 2 hours, or until set.

4 For the jelly, dissolve the gelatine in 4 tablespoons of water as in Step 1. Cool for 10 minutes. Add the wine and icing sugar and stir well. Pour over the mousses. Chill for 1 hour, or until the jelly is set. Serve.

Step 2

Step 3

Step 4

Preparation: **30** Min Chilling: **3** Hours
Per Serving: 150 kcal/631 kJ;
8g protein; 3g fat; 20g carbohydrate

TYPICALLY SWEDISH

The nine northern provinces of Sweden are known collectively as Norrland and have a cold, almost arctic climate. Wild berries, such as arctic raspberries and cloudberries, grow here and are used in preserves for meat and game, as well as delicate cakes and desserts.

Cooking tip

Make sure the gelatine is completely dissolved in the water before using. Dip in a clean teaspoon — there should be no granules on the back. If it is not dissolved, return the bowl to the pan for a few more minutes.

Serving tip

Serve a selection of cold dishes before the mousse, such as smoked salmon strips, large prawns, mini meatballs, rollmop herrings and cold meats. Add lemon wedges, dill sprigs and bowls of mayonnaise and cranberry sauce for dipping.

SERVING TIP These fruit puffs are best served warm. Drizzle them with a little single cream, or accompany with a scoop of vanilla ice cream or lemon sorbet for a cool contrast.

BLACKBERRY AND APPLE PUFFS

THE NETHERLANDS

INGREDIENTS

(Makes 6 puffs)

- 250g/9oz puff pastry
- beaten egg, to glaze
- caster sugar, to sprinkle

FOR THE FILLING

- 350g/12oz cooking apples
- 40g/1½oz caster sugar
- 15g/½oz butter
- 100g/4oz blackberries

INGREDIENTS TIP

Fresh, frozen or tinned blackberries all work well in this recipe. If using frozen or tinned berries, drain them well before adding to the apple mixture.

A favourite fruit combination is given a new look in these flaky pastry parcels. And you don't have to wait for the blackberry season — use tinned or frozen fruit and make them any time.

1 For the filling, peel, core and slice the apples. Put them into a saucepan with the sugar, butter and 2 tablespoons of cold water. Cover and simmer for 5 minutes, or until the apples are tender and the water has evaporated. Leave to cool completely, then stir in the blackberries.

Step 2

2 Preheat the oven to 200°C/400°F/Gas 6. Lightly grease two baking sheets. Roll out the pastry on a lightly floured surface to form a 38x25cm/15x10in rectangle. Using a sharp knife, cut the pastry into six 12.5cm/5in squares.

Step 3

3 Divide the fruit mixture between the squares, spooning it into the centre of each one. Dampen the pastry edges with water and fold in half to make triangles. Press down the edges to seal.

Step 4

4 Transfer the triangles to the prepared baking sheets. Brush all over with egg and sprinkle generously with caster sugar. Bake for 20–25 minutes, or until puffed up and pale golden. Serve warm.

Preparation: **20** Min Cooking: **25** Min
Per Puff: 234 kcal/982 kJ;
3g protein; 12g fat; 30g carbohydrate

TYPICALLY DUTCH

Windmills are a common site, particularly in the northern areas of Holland where a strong sea wind blows much of the time. As most of the country is below sea level, the power produced by the windmills is used for land drainage schemes to prevent flooding.

HIGHLAND BERRY CREAM

GREAT BRITAIN

INGREDIENTS

(Serves 4)

- 4 tbsp clear honey
- 3 tbsp whisky
- 284ml/10fl oz whipping cream
- 350g/12oz raspberries
- 2x40g/1½oz muesli bars

INGREDIENTS TIP

Use crisp muesli bars rather than chewy ones for this recipe to give a tasty contrast of textures. Miniature bottles of Scotch whisky are available from off licences and some supermarkets if you don't want to buy a full-size bottle. Or omit the alcohol and add the same quantity of orange juice instead.

These pretty layered desserts couldn't be easier to make. Combining three favourite Scottish ingredients — honey, raspberries and whisky — they're sure to please.

1 Put the honey, whisky and cream in a large mixing bowl. Whisk with an electric mixer or by hand with a balloon whisk until soft peaks form — the tips should flop over when you lift the whisk from the bowl.

Step 1

2 Spoon a third of the raspberries into the base of four serving glasses or dishes. Spoon half the cream mixture on top.

Step 2

3 Put the muesli bars into a strong plastic food bag and crush to crumbs with a rolling pin. Alternatively, put in a food processor. Using the metal blade, pulse until the bars break into crumbs. Scatter half the crumbs over the cream in the glasses. Add half the remaining raspberries.

4 Repeat the layers of cream, muesli and raspberries to complete the desserts. Chill for 30 minutes in the fridge before serving.

Step 3

Preparation: **10** Min Chilling: **30** Min
Per Serving: 463 kcal/1922 kJ;
5g protein; 33g fat; 34g carbohydrate

TYPICALLY SCOTTISH

Country dancing has been a favourite pastime in Scotland since the 16th century. The most well-known dances are the reel and the Highland fling — a solo dance performed every year at the start of the national Highland games.

OOKING TIP

ou can use fresh or frozen raspberries for these esserts. If using frozen, thaw them first on a plate ned with a double thickness of kitchen paper to ak up the excess moisture. Gently pat the fruit ry with more kitchen paper before using.

SERVING TIP

Neeps (mashed potato, carrot and red turnips seasoned with pepper) is a traditional Scottish accompaniment for haggis. It also goes well with roast meat, such as beef, lamb or pork. Finish the meal with these simple desserts, and a generous measure of whisky.

BLACKBERRY ROULADE

NORWAY

This favourite Scandinavian dessert makes good use of frozen blackberries, encasing them in a wonderfully light nutty sponge roll. Serve with whipped cream for an extra indulgence.

INGREDIENTS
(Makes 8 slices)

- 150g/5oz plain flour
- 50g/2oz ground pecan nuts
- 4 large eggs
- 1 tsp vanilla essence
- 150g/5oz caster sugar, plus extra to sprinkle
- ¼ tsp cream of tartar

FOR THE FILLING

- 450g/1lb frozen blackberries, thawed
- 50g/2oz caster sugar
- 1 tbsp cornflour
- 1 tsp lemon juice
- blackberries and mint sprigs, to decorate

INGREDIENTS TIP
Buy shelled pecan nuts and grind them yourself in a food processor or coffee grinder. If you don't have a processor or grinder, use ready-ground almonds or hazelnuts instead.

1 For the filling, drain berries and reserve the juice. Put juice, sugar, cornflour and lemon juice in a pan. Heat gently until thick. Transfer to a bowl; stir in the berries. Cool.

2 Preheat the oven to 180°C/350°F/Gas 4. Grease a large Swiss roll tin and line with non-stick baking paper. Sift the flour into a bowl; stir in the nuts. Separate the eggs. Beat the yolks, vanilla and half the sugar with an electric whisk until the beaters leave a trail when lifted. Whisk in the flour mixture.

3 In a clean bowl, whisk the egg whites until foamy. Whisk in the remaining sugar and cream of tartar until stiff. Carefully fold the egg whites into the egg yolk mixture. Spoon into the tin and level the surface.

4 Bake for 10 minutes, or until golden. Put a sheet of baking paper on a tea towel; sprinkle with sugar. Turn out sponge onto the paper; remove the lining paper. Trim the edges. Roll up the sponge (see Cooking tip).

5 Unroll the sponge. Spread filling down the middle, leaving a 2.5cm/1in border. Re-roll the sponge; put on a plate. Dust with caster sugar and serve with berries and mint.

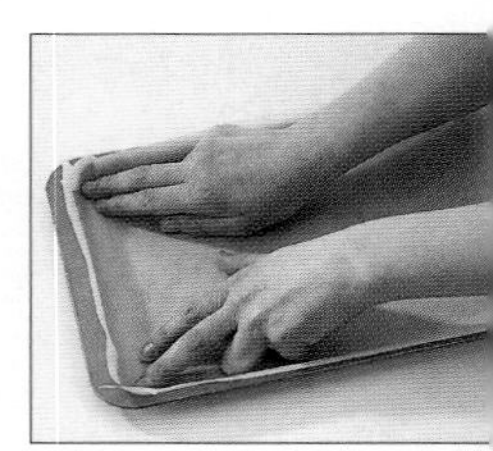

Step 2

Step 2

Step 4

Preparation: 45 Min
Cooking: 10 Min, plus cooling
Per Slice: 281 kcal/1185 kJ;
7g protein; 8g fat; 48g carbohydrate

TYPICALLY NORWEGIAN
Fjords are an integral part of the dramatic landscape of Norway. These waterways are used for local travel as well as to connect inland areas with the coastal ports. High-speed boats and tourist ferries have now replaced the traditional rowing boats.

OOKING TIPS

oll up the sponge with the sugared paper, using
e tea towel as a guide. Put the roll seam-side
own on a wire rack and leave to cool. Unroll and
move the paper • The sponge is cooked when it
s turned pale golden and the centre springs back
hen pressed gently with a finger.

SERVING TIP

For a Norwegian main course, serve grilled mackerel with a tangy gooseberry sauce and slices of brown bread. Plain boiled potatoes are the traditional accompaniment. Serve the roulade for dessert with lightly whipped cream or crème fraîche.

SERVING TIP Serve the slice after a main course of creamy risotto flavoured with mushrooms, fresh herbs and thin slices of cooked chicken. Add a loaf of crusty bread to soak up the delicious juices.

RASPBERRY SLICE

NORTHERN ITALY

Evaporated milk adds a luscious creaminess to this fruity slice while its rich flavour blends beautifully with the tangy berries. It's so tempting, no one will be able to refuse a second slice.

INGREDIENTS

(Makes 10 slices)

- 100g/4oz digestive biscuits
- 50g/2oz hazelnuts
- 50g/2oz butter
- 2 tbsp caster sugar

FOR THE TOPPING

- 1 packet raspberry jelly
- 170g/6oz can evaporated milk, chilled
- 150g/5oz natural yoghurt
- 225g/8oz raspberries

FOR THE DECORATION

- 142ml/5fl oz double cream
- 1 tsp caster sugar
- few drops vanilla essence
- 25g/1oz hazelnuts

INGREDIENTS TIP

Evaporated milk is twice as concentrated as ordinary milk. It has a thick creamy texture and a rich flavour, making it ideal for desserts and milk puddings.

1 Line a 20cm/8in loose-bottomed square tin with non-PVC cling film, allowing some to overhang the edges. For the topping, put the jelly into a pan with 150ml/¼ pint water and heat gently until the jelly dissolves. Pour into a bowl and leave to cool.

2 Meanwhile, put the biscuits into a plastic bag, seal and tap with a rolling pin until crushed. Chop 50g/2oz of hazelnuts. Melt the butter. Mix the biscuits, nuts, butter and 2 tablespoons of caster sugar and press into the base of the tin. Chill until required.

Step 2

3 Put the evaporated milk into a large bowl. Beat with an electric whisk until trebled in volume and the beaters leave a trail on the surface when lifted. Whisk in the yoghurt and cooled jelly until blended. Stir in the raspberries. Pour into the tin and level the surface. Chill for 30 minutes, or until firm.

Step 3

4 For the decoration, whip the cream with the sugar and vanilla until soft peaks form. Spoon into a piping bag fitted with a star-shaped nozzle. Carefully remove the dessert from the tin and cut into slices. Pipe 2 cream rosettes on each slice. Halve the hazelnuts and put on top of the rosettes.

Step 4

Preparation: 30 Min, plus cooling and chilling
Per Slice: 285 kcal/1186 kJ;
5g protein; 20g fat; 24g carbohydrate

TYPICALLY ITALIAN

The Roman amphitheatre at Verona was built in AD30 to stage huge gladiatorial contests. With seating for 20,000 people, it shows the importance of the city in ancient times. Nowadays, it is the setting for a world famous summer festival of opera.

RASPBERRY CINNAMON TORTE

AUSTRIA

The Austrians are renowned for their fabulous pastries and cakes. This warm cinnamon-scented sponge, with a secret layer of tangy raspberries hidden inside, is a perfect example.

INGREDIENTS

(Makes 8 slices)

- 175g/6oz softened butter
- 175g/6oz soft brown sugar
- 3 eggs
- 175g/6oz self-raising flour
- 175g/6oz ground almonds
- 1 tsp ground cinnamon
- 2 tbsp milk
- 275g/10oz raspberries
- icing sugar, to dust

INGREDIENTS TIP

Take the butter out of the fridge about 30 minutes before you start to make the cake. This gives it plenty of time to soften so it blends easily with the other ingredients.

1 Preheat the oven to 180°C/350°F/Gas 4. Line the base of a 23cm/9in spring-form cake tin with non-stick baking paper.

Step 1

2 Put the butter and brown sugar in a large mixing bowl. Beat with an electric mixer or wooden spoon until soft and creamy. Gradually beat in the eggs. Beat in the flour, almonds, cinnamon and milk to make a soft dropping consistency.

3 Spread half the mixture in the base of the prepared tin. Spoon over the raspberries. Top with the remaining cake mixture. Spread the top level with the back of a spoon.

Step 3

4 Bake the cake for 35 minutes, or until risen, golden and firm to the touch. Allow to cool in the tin for 10 minutes, then turn out onto a serving plate. Arrange strips of non-stick baking paper in a lattice pattern over the top of the cake. Dust with icing sugar to make a checked pattern. Carefully remove the paper and serve the cake warm.

Step 4

Preparation: **20** Min
Cooking: **35** Min, plus cooling
Per Slice: 496 kcal/2061 kJ;
10g protein; 33g fat; 44g carbohydrate

TYPICALLY AUSTRIAN

As well as the many coffee houses serving fresh cakes and hot drinks, Austria has a wealth of pâtisseries which are worth a visit. Along with classic cakes like Sachertorte and Gugelhopf, you can always find the favourite national dessert, apple strudel.

Cooking tips

To save on preparation time, make the cake in a food processor. Put all the ingredients, except the berries, into the processor and blend until smooth and combined • For a sauce to serve with the cake, purée 300g/10oz raspberries with juice of 1 orange. Sieve, then sweeten to taste with icing sugar.

Serving tip

For a main course, serve a selection of cold meats and fish. Arrange them on a platter with green and red lettuce leaves, slices of cucumber and whole cherry tomatoes. Serve the warm cake with raspberry sauce (see Cooking tip) or cream.

3 WAYS WITH CHEESECAKES

Frozen mixed summer berries mean you can enjoy any of these deliciously rich cheesecakes all year round.

ALMOND BERRY CHEESECAKE

Preparation: **30** Min, plus overnight chilling

SOUTHERN FRANCE

(SERVES 8)

- 75g/3oz butter
- 175g/6oz almond biscuits
- 500g/1lb 2oz frozen mixed summer berries, thawed
- 1 sachet powdered gelatine
- 225g/8oz cream cheese
- 200g/7oz crème fraîche
- 2 eggs, separated
- 75g/3oz caster sugar
- strawberries and icing sugar, to decorate

1 Melt the butter and crush the biscuits. Mix together and spread over the base of a 20cm/8in spring-form cake tin. Chill. Drain the berries, reserving 4 tablespoons of juice. Sprinkle gelatine over juice and leave until spongy. Stand bowl in a pan of hot water until dissolved, stirring.

2 Whisk cheese, crème fraîche, egg yolks and sugar until smooth. Add gelatine mixture in a steady stream, whisking until combined. Fold in the berries.

3 Whisk egg whites until stiff. Fold into berry mixture. Pour into tin and spread level. Chill overnight until set. Turn out cake and decorate with halved strawberries and icing sugar.

BERRY SOUFFI

Preparation: **30** M

GERMANY

(SERVES 8)

- 75g/3oz butter
- 175g/6oz digestive biscuits
- 500g/1lb 2oz frozen mixed summer berries, thawed
- 3 eggs, separated
- 175g/6oz caster sugar
- 450g/1lb quark or low fat curd cheese
- 40g/1½oz plain flour

1 Preheat the oven to 180°C/350°F/Gas 4. Melt the butter and crush the digestive biscuits. Mix together and spread over base of a 20cm/8in spring-form cake tin. Chill. Drain the berries in a sieve.

·HEESECAKE

›oking: **1** Hour Cooling: **1** Hour

2 Whisk the egg yolks and sugar until thick and creamy and the whisk leaves a trail on the surface when lifted. Beat the quark or curd cheese until soft. Fold the egg mixture and flour into the cheese. Fold in the berries.

3 Whisk the egg whites until stiff peaks form. Carefully old into the berry mixture. Pour into the tin and spread evel. Bake for 1 hour, or intil firm. Cool for 1 hour n the turned off oven with ne door ajar.

4 Carefully turn out the cheese-cake and transfer to a serving ·late. Serve straight away.

CHOCOLATE BERRY CHEESECAKE

Preparation: **30** Min Cooking: **1½** Hours

USA

(SERVES 8)

- **500g/1lb 2oz frozen mixed summer berries, thawed**
- **175g/6oz plain flour**
- **40g/1½oz cocoa, plus extra to dust**
- **75g/3oz butter**
- **100g/4oz caster sugar**
- **2 eggs, plus 1 egg yolk**
- **450g/1lb cream cheese**
- **142ml/5fl oz sour cream**
- **blueberries, to decorate**

1 Preheat oven to 170°C/325°F/Gas 3. Drain berries in a sieve.

2 Sift flour and 15g/½oz cocoa into a bowl. Rub in the butter with your fingers to form fine crumbs. Stir in 25g/1oz sugar and 1 egg yolk to make a soft dough. Roll out the dough and use to line a 20cm/8in spring-form cake tin. Chill until required.

3 Whisk 2 egg yolks with the remaining sugar until the whisk leaves a trail on the surface when lifted. Whisk in the cheese, cream and cocoa. Fold in berries.

4 Whisk egg whites until stiff. Fold into the cheese mixture. Spoon into tin and spread level. Bake for 1½ hours, or until risen and just set. Decorate with the blueberries, dust with cocoa and serve hot.

*F*RUIT MERINGUE CRUSH

SOUTHERN ITALY

Luscious dark cherries with layers of crisp meringue and smooth cream combine in these irresistible Italian specialities. Sweet and tangy passion-fruit adds an attractive finishing touch.

INGREDIENTS

(Makes 4 desserts)

- 284ml/10fl oz pot extra-thick double cream
- 275g/10oz Greek-style yoghurt
- 3 tbsp icing sugar
- 2 tbsp crème de cassis
- 4 ready-made meringue nests
- 2 passion-fruit
- 450g/1lb canned black or red cherries

INGREDIENTS TIP

Crème de cassis is a liqueur made from blackcurrants and has an intense fruit flavour. You can use other liqueurs for a change. Try cherry or apricot brandy, raspberry liqueur (crème de framboise) or Amaretto (almond liqueur).

1 Put the thick cream and yoghurt into a mixing bowl and stir together. Sift over the icing sugar and gently fold in, along with the crème de cassis, until just blended.

2 Put the meringue nests into a plastic food bag and crush into pieces with a rolling pin. Cut the passion-fruit in half and use a teaspoon to scoop out the seeds and pulp into a dish.

3 Spoon the cherries and their juice into four dessert glasses. Top with half the cream mixture, crushed meringues and passion-fruit.

4 Repeat the layers, finishing with passion-fruit on top. Put the glasses into the fridge and chill for 1 hour before serving.

Step 1

Step 2

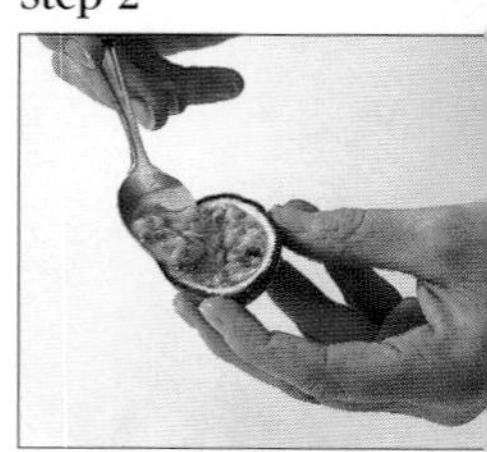

Step 2

Preparation: **10** Min Chilling: **1** Hour
Per Dessert: 661 kcal/2748 kJ;
8g protein; 41g fat; 66g carbohydrate

TYPICALLY ROMAN

Roman cuisine was traditionally based around the noble principles of prudence and temperance; the recipes were followed carefully with no improvisation. Many ancient recipes still survive but attitudes are more casual with the growth in popularity of fast food.

OOKING TIPS

on't overbeat the cream mixture when folding in e icing sugar and crème de cassis or it will turn nny and won't stay in layers in the dishes • For a fferent look, spoon the cream mixture into 4 large 8 smaller meringue nests. Top with the cherries d passion-fruit and serve straight away.

SERVING TIP

For an Italian meal, start with a vegetable soup flavoured with tomatoes, cauliflower, carrots and courgettes. Follow with chunky meatballs in a tomato and basil sauce served with spaghetti or diced sautéed potatoes and broccoli.

SERVING TIP A main course of grilled salmon or tuna steaks brushed with herby olive oil would be ideal before this dessert. Serve the fish with potato salad or buttered new potatoes, and mixed leaves.

STRAWBERRY ALMOND DESSERTS

SOUTHERN ITALY

INGREDIENTS

(Makes 6 desserts)

- 2 egg whites
- 75g/3oz caster sugar
- 40g/1½oz ground almonds
- 350g/12oz strawberries

FOR THE PRALINE CREAM

- 50g/2oz granulated sugar
- 50g/2oz blanched almonds
- 284ml/10fl oz pot double cream

INGREDIENTS TIP

Blanched almonds have had their skins removed. If you can't find ready-blanched nuts, you can remove the brown skins yourself. Pour boiling water over the shelled nuts and leave for a few minutes. Drain well. When cool enough to handle, just rub off the skins with your fingers.

Almonds are a favourite ingredient in Italian desserts. In this recipe, they flavour the nutty meringue and sweet praline cream that make up these tempting strawberry sundaes.

1 Preheat the oven to 110°C/225°F/Gas ¼. Line a 27x18cm/11x7in baking tin with non-stick baking paper. Whisk the egg whites until stiff peaks form. Gradually whisk in the caster sugar. Fold in the ground almonds. Spoon the mixture into the tin and spread level. Bake for 2 hours, or until crisp. Cool.

Step 1

2 Meanwhile, make the praline cream. Oil a baking tin. Put the sugar and blanched almonds into a saucepan with 2 tablespoons of water. Cook over a low heat until the sugar melts. Increase the heat and cook, without stirring, until clear and golden. Pour onto the oiled tray and leave to set.

Step 2

3 Hull and slice the strawberries. When set, break the praline into pieces, put into a food processor and crush into crumbs. Whip the cream to a soft dropping consistency. Reserve 1 tablespoon of praline and fold the remainder into the cream.

Step 3

4 Break the meringue into pieces. Arrange half in the base of six dessert glasses. Add half the cream, then half the berries. Repeat the layers, reserving a few strawberry slices to decorate. Chill for 30 minutes. Top with the reserved praline and strawberries.

eparation: **30** Min
ooking: **2** Hours, plus setting
hilling: **30** Min
er Dessert: 407 kcal/1691 kJ;
g protein; 31g fat; 28g carbohydrate

TYPICALLY SICILIAN

Almonds trees flourish in the warm climate of Sicily, and the nuts they produce feature heavily in the island's cuisine. Almond nougat, sugary marzipan and rich ricotta desserts satisfy the sweet tooth while nutty chicken stews and fish dishes are also popular.

SUMMER BERRY COMPOTE

CANADA

This luscious midsummer dessert is simple to make from any red fruits that are available. And it's low in fat, so you can even go back for guilt-free second helpings.

INGREDIENTS

(Serves 4)

- 700g/1½lb mixed red fruits, e.g. strawberries, raspberries, redcurrants, loganberries and tayberries
- 100g/4oz caster sugar
- 2 tsp arrowroot

INGREDIENTS TIP

Arrowroot is a fine white powder used for thickening sauces. It turns clear when mixed with liquid, so gives a less cloudy result than using cornflour.

1 Prepare the mixed fruits. Wash, hull and halve the strawberries. Remove the redcurrants from their stalks using the prongs of a fork. Remove any leaves or stalks from the other berries.

Step 1

2 Put the sugar into a pan with 450ml/ ¾ pint of water. Heat gently, stirring, until the sugar dissolves. Bring to the boil.

Step 2

3 Add the redcurrants to the pan and cook for 4 minutes. Add the strawberries, raspberries, loganberries or tayberries and cook for 3–5 minutes, or until softened.

4 Mix the arrowroot to a smooth paste with 1 tablespoon of water and stir into the fruit. Cook, stirring, until the mixture thickens, then remove from the heat. Serve warm or chilled.

Step 4

Preparation: **15** Min Cooking: **10** Min
Per Serving: 149 kcal/632 kJ;
2g protein; 0.2g fat; 37g carbohydrate

TYPICALLY CANADIAN

Canada's Alberta province is a fertile area of large, sweeping plains bordered by snow-capped mountains. The country's finest lamb and beef originates here, as well as quality wheat. The cuisine is plain and filling, with steaks, beans and stews featuring heavily.

‹OOKING TIPS

or a special treat, add a tablespoon of liqueur, such
ˌ crème de cassis or kirsch, to the compote before
:irring in the arrowroot paste • For a decoration,
ˌvirl a spoonful of thick cream, Greek-style yoghurt
ɾ fromage frais into each bowl of compote.

SERVING TIP

Serve a filling main course before this simple fruity dessert. Fry bacon and eggs and serve on hot toasted and buttered muffins or bagels. Add some fried potato and onion slices for a really hearty meal.

Serving tip Serve the pie warm or cold with whipped or pouring cream. Stir some finely grated lemon rind into the cream to complement the lemon flavouring in the filling.

CANADIAN BLUEBERRY PIE

CANADA

This lemony lattice-topped pie is a favourite all over Canada. If you don't have a spring-form cake tin, you can bake it in a normal cake tin or a ceramic pie dish set on a baking tray.

INGREDIENTS

(Serves 6)

- 275g/10oz plain flour
- pinch of salt
- 100g/4oz butter
- 75g/3oz caster sugar
- 1 egg

FOR THE FILLING

- 1 lemon
- 250g/9oz fresh blueberries
- 50g/2oz caster sugar
- 25g/1oz butter
- 40g/1½oz cornflour

INGREDIENTS TIP

If you can't find fresh blueberries, use raspberries instead. For a nutty pastry, replace 50g/2oz of the flour with ground almonds and add a few drops of almond essence to the mixture.

1 Sift the flour and salt into a bowl. Rub in 100g/4oz butter to make fine crumbs. Stir in 75g/3oz sugar. Add the egg and 2 teaspoons water and mix to form a soft dough. Wrap in non-PVC cling film and chill for 20 minutes. Preheat oven to 200°C/400°F/Gas 6.

Step 1

2 Meanwhile, make the filling. Grate the rind and squeeze the juice from the lemon. Put into a pan with the blueberries, sugar, butter and cornflour. Slowly bring to the boil, stirring, and cook for 1–2 minutes until thickened. Set aside to cool.

3 Roll out two-thirds of the pastry and use to line the base and two-thirds up the side of a 20cm/8in spring-form cake tin. Line with baking paper and weight down with baking beans. Bake for 10 minutes. Remove the beans and paper and bake for 5 minutes. Reduce the oven heat to 180°C/350°F/Gas 4.

Step 3

4 Spoon the filling into the pastry case. Roll out the remaining pastry and cut into 1cm/½in wide strips. Arrange over the filling in a lattice pattern. Bake for 15–20 minutes, or until the pastry is golden. Cool in the tin for 10 minutes, then remove side of the tin and put the pie on a serving plate.

Step 4

Preparation: **30** Min Chilling: **20** Min
Cooking: **35** Min
Per Serving: 457 kcal/1922 kJ;
6g protein; 19g fat; 70g carbohydrate

TYPICALLY QUEBEC

Québec City, overlooking the St Lawrence Seaway, was founded by French traders in 1608. The city, particularly the old quarter, is a maze of narrow winding streets where quaint inns and cafés nestle among the stone churches and copper-topped houses.

STRAWBERRY INDULGENCE

CANADA

INGREDIENTS

(Serves 4)

- 450g/1lb fresh strawberries
- 5 tbsp icing sugar
- 3 tbsp kirsch, optional
- 375g/13oz mascarpone cheese
- mint sprigs, to decorate

INGREDIENTS TIP

Mascarpone is a soft Italian cream cheese with a smooth texture and decadently rich flavour. Used in desserts and some savoury dishes to add richness, it can also be served with cakes and fruit pies instead of cream or crème fraîche.

Strawberries are a favourite fruit all over Canada. This super-easy recipe makes a lovely alternative to plain strawberries and cream, and it looks gorgeous too.

1 Wash and hull the strawberries. Pat them dry on kitchen paper. Reserve a few berries for decoration then mash the rest together with the icing sugar and kirsch, if using. Push the mixture through a sieve to make a smooth purée.

2 Put the mascarpone cheese in a large mixing bowl. Add half the strawberry purée. Beat with an electric whisk until smooth, thick and combined.

3 Lightly fold the remaining purée into the mascarpone mixture, without over mixing, to give a marbled effect.

4 Divide the mixture between four dessert bowls. Chill for 20 minutes. Halve the reserved strawberries. Serve the desserts garnished with mint and berries.

Step 2

Step 2

Step 3

Preparation: **10** Min Chilling: **20** Min
Per Serving: 550 kcal/2301 kJ;
4g protein; 44g fat; 37g carbohydrate

TYPICALLY CANADIAN

Strawberries are grown in every province of Canada but Manitoba is considered the berry capital. Every year in July the National Strawberry Festival is held here with shows, markets, games and activities and, of course, plenty of delicious strawberries and cream.

Cooking tip

Fold the strawberry purée gently into the mascarpone mixture with a large metal spoon. Turn the bowl so the spoon scoops the sides, then make a cutting action through the centre of the mixture. Swirl the mixtures to create a marbled pattern but don't overmix or the colourful effect will be lost.

Serving tip

For a light summer meal, serve a mixed leaf salad with cranberries, crispy bacon and chunks of blue cheese, such as dolcelatte. Dress with olive oil, lemon juice and salt and pepper. Finish with these creamy desserts served with almond biscuits.

*T*WO-TONE STRAWBERRY JELLIES

NEW ZEALAND

INGREDIENTS

(Serves 4)

- 1 sachet powdered gelatine
- 400g/14oz can coconut milk
- 25g/1oz granulated sugar
- 1 packet strawberry jelly
- 225g/8oz fresh strawberries
- 142ml/5fl oz pot whipping cream, optional

INGREDIENTS TIP

Coconut milk is made from the coconut flesh and has a creamy but not overly rich flavour. As well as being used in both sweet and savoury dishes, it makes a terrific addition to a summery cocktail with fruit juice and rum.

No longer just a party treat for children, these sophisticated jellies contain an exotic pairing of coconut and strawberries — and the two-tone effect is easier to create than it looks.

1 Sprinkle the gelatine over 90ml/3fl oz of water in a cup or small bowl. Leave until spongy. Stand the cup or bowl in a pan of hot water until the gelatine dissolves. Put into a large bowl with the coconut milk. Whisk in the sugar until combined.

2 Pour the coconut mixture into four tall glasses. Put them in the fridge resting against an egg carton so the mixture lies at an angle. Leave for 2 hours, or until set.

3 Make up the jelly in a jug with 600ml/1 pint of water, following the packet instructions. Leave to cool. Wash, hull and slice the strawberries.

4 Put the glasses in a roasting tin. Arrange the sliced berries in the glasses and carefully pour in the jelly. Return the glasses to the fridge on the tray, standing upright, and chill for 2 hours, or until set.

5 Whip the cream, if using, until soft peaks form and use to decorate the jellies. Serve straight from the fridge.

Step 1

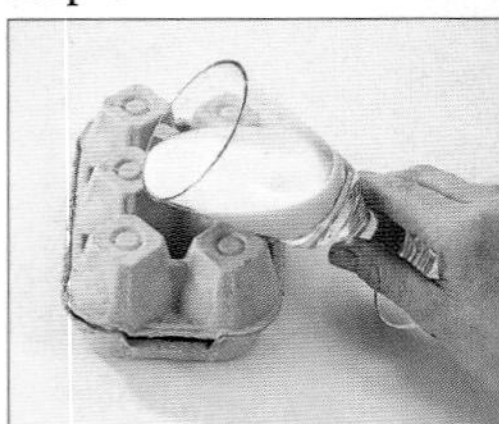

Step 2

Step 4

Preparation: **10** Min Chilling: **4** Hours

Per Serving: 282 kcal/1173 kJ;
6g protein; 14g fat; 35g carbohydrate

TYPICALLY NEW ZEALAND

Bay of Islands on the North Island is one of New Zealand's most popular holiday areas. As well as favourite outdoor activities like sailing, diving and fishing, visitors can enjoy a swim with dolphins or a boat trip through the spectacular 'hole in the rock'.

OOKING TIPS

he strawberry jelly must be cold but not fully set
vhen you pour it into the glasses with the coconut
nixture • An empty egg box is ideal for leaning the
lasses against so that the coconut jelly sets at an
ngle. Make sure it is completely set before adding
ne strawberry jelly or the effect will be lost.

SERVING TIP

Small rib lamb chops make a delicious main course with a mint and vinegar dipping sauce. Add boiled new potatoes tossed with butter and mint and a green vegetable, such as mange tout or peas.

SERVING TIP For a luxurious finish, use a potato peeler to shave curls of plain or white chocolate from a large bar. Keep them in a cool place and scatter them on top of the fruit just before serving.

THREE BERRY PAVLOVA

AUSTRALIA

Meltingly soft inside and crisp to the bite on the outside, this classic meringue dessert is a firm favourite. A simple topping of mixed berries adds a colourful splash to the dinner table.

INGREDIENTS

(Serves 4)

- 3 egg whites
- 175g/6oz caster sugar
- ½ tsp vanilla essence
- ½ tsp white wine vinegar
- 1 tsp cornflour

FOR THE FILLING

- 284ml/10fl oz pot double cream
- 225g/8oz strawberries
- 100g/4oz raspberries
- 100g/4oz blueberries

INGREDIENTS TIP

For an extra fruity flavour, purée 75g/3oz raspberries and stir into the whipped cream before spooning over the Pavlova.

1 Preheat the oven to 150°C/300°F/Gas 2. Cut an 18cm/7in circle out of non-stick baking paper. Put on a baking sheet.

2 Whisk the egg whites until stiff peaks form. Add half the caster sugar, the vanilla essence, vinegar and cornflour. Whisk again until stiff. Gradually whisk in the remaining sugar until thick and glossy.

Step 2

3 Using a large spoon, place spoonfuls of meringue over the baking paper circle, covering it completely. Bake for 1 hour, or until the meringue is crisp. Leave to cool completely on the baking sheet.

Step 3

4 For the filling, whip the cream until it forms soft peaks. Remove the meringue from the baking sheet. Peel off the baking paper and put the meringue on a serving plate. Spoon over the cream. Halve the strawberries and scatter evenly on top, along with the raspberries and blueberries. Serve immediately.

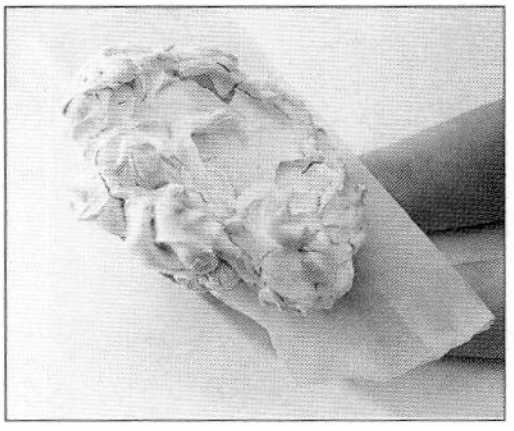

Step 4

-eparation: **20** Min
ooking: **1** Hour, plus cooling
-r Serving: 535 kcal/2234 kJ;
; protein; 34g fat; 56g carbohydrate

TYPICALLY AUSTRALIAN

Australia is renowned for its golden beaches and excellent surfing. Tourists and locals flock to the coast to enjoy swimming, surfing or just relaxing and sunbathing on the sands. Keen surfers arrive at sunrise hoping to catch the biggest waves before anyone else.

CLASSIC STRAWBERRY SHORTCAKES

USA

Modern versions of this American dessert often use a sponge cake, but this classic shortcake, as its name suggests, is 'short' or crisp, halfway between a cake and a biscuit.

INGREDIENTS
(Makes 6 shortcakes)

- 350g/12oz plain flour
- pinch of salt
- 1½ tsp baking powder
- 75g/3oz butter
- 150ml/¼ pint milk
- 1 egg yolk
- ½ tsp vanilla essence
- beaten egg or milk, to glaze
- 1 tbsp caster sugar
- 25g/1oz flaked almonds
- icing sugar, to dust

FOR THE FILLING

- 700g/1½lb strawberries
- 50–75g/2–3oz caster sugar
- 6 scoops ice cream

INGREDIENTS TIP

You can use any flavour ice cream. Vanilla is the classic American choice but raspberry ripple, strawberry and lemon sorbet make good alternatives. Otherwise, fill cakes with whipped cream.

1 For the filling, hull and halve the strawberries. Put in a bowl with caster sugar to taste. Crush a few of the berries with a fork. Cover and leave to stand for 30 minutes.

Step 1

2 Preheat the oven to 220°C/425°F/Gas 7. Grease 2 large baking sheets. Sift the flour, salt and baking powder into a bowl. Dice the butter and rub in to form fine crumbs. Mix the milk, egg and vanilla; stir into the flour mixture to form a dough.

3 Turn out the dough onto a lightly floured surface and knead gently until smooth. Divide the dough into 6 pieces and roll into balls. Flatten each one out into a 7.5cm/3in round and put on the baking sheets.

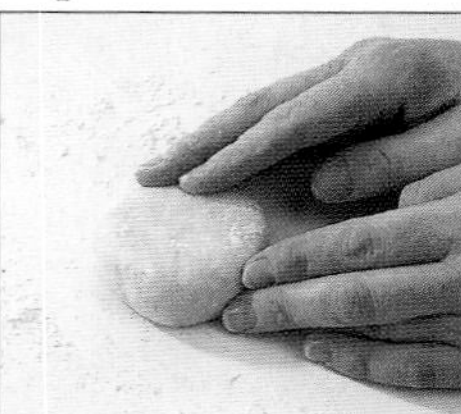

Step 3

4 Brush the dough rounds with egg or milk. Scatter over the caster sugar and almonds. Bake for 12–15 minutes, or until well risen and golden brown.

Step 4

5 Transfer the shortcakes to a wire rack and dust with icing sugar. Cut each one in half while still warm. Put the bottom halves into serving dishes. Spoon over some strawberries and add a scoop of ice cream. Top with the remaining shortcake halves.

Preparation: **20** Min Standing: **30** Min
Cooking: **15** Min
Per Shortcake: 553 kcal/2324 kJ;
11g protein; 22g fat; 83g carbohydrate

TYPICALLY AMERICAN

The beautiful scenery of New England is at its best in the autumn or fall when the leaves turn to vivid reds, yellows and oranges. The colourful trees provide the perfect contrast to the simple wooden Shaker-style houses and churches that dot the countryside.

Cooking tips

You can use either egg or milk to glaze the shortcakes. Beaten egg will give a more golden finish when baked • Shortcake is best served warm, fresh from the oven. If you have to make it ahead, warm the cakes briefly in a medium oven before adding the filling and serving.

Serving tip

A light main course of pan-fried turkey breast and watercress salad is ideal before these sweet shortcakes. For extra flavour, marinate the turkey in oil, lime juice and chopped mixed herbs for a couple of hours before frying.

PEACH AND BERRY COBBLER

USA

Cobblers have been a popular family dessert in America since the mid-1800s. In this simple recipe, pretty heart-shaped scones top the bubbling sweet fruit filling.

INGREDIENTS

(Serves 6)

- 3 peaches
- 1 tsp cornflour
- 3 tbsp caster sugar
- 150ml/¼ pint orange juice
- 450g/1lb raspberries
- 225g/8oz blackberries

FOR THE TOPPING

- 225g/8oz plain flour
- 1 tsp baking powder
- ½ tsp ground nutmeg
- 50g/2oz butter
- 40g/1½oz caster sugar
- 1 egg
- 2–3 tbsp milk
- icing sugar, to dust

INGREDIENTS TIP

You can vary the fruits used for the cobbler. Try apricots, apples, pears or nectarines. You can also use a 400g/14oz can of peaches, if you can't find fresh ones.

1 Preheat the oven to 200°C/400°F/Gas 6. Peel, stone and chop the peaches. Put the cornflour and 3 tablespoons of caster sugar in a pan and mix together. Add the peaches and orange juice. Simmer over a medium heat for 5 minutes, stirring frequently, until the mixture thickens.

Step 2

2 Add the raspberries and blackberries to the pan and stir to mix. Spoon the mixture into a 1.2 litre/2 pint ovenproof dish.

Step 3

3 For the topping, sift the flour, baking powder and nutmeg into a large mixing bowl. Dice the butter and rub in with your fingertips until the mixture resembles fine crumbs. Stir in the sugar.

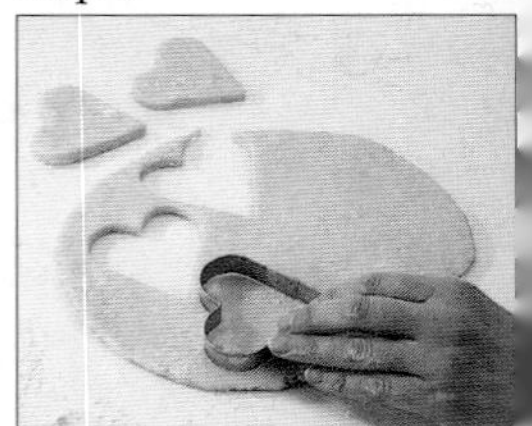

Step 4

4 Beat the egg and add to the bowl with enough milk to make a soft, not sticky dough. Roll out the dough on a floured surface until about 1cm/½in thick. Stamp out six scones with a heart-shaped or a 7.5cm/3in round cutter. Arrange on top of the fruit.

5 Bake the cobbler for 20–25 minutes, or until the scones are golden and well risen and the fruit is bubbling. Dust with icing sugar and serve hot.

Preparation: **20** Min Cooking: **25** Min
Per Serving: 335 kcal/1411 kJ;
7g protein; 9g fat; 61g carbohydrate

TYPICALLY AMERICAN

Elvis's Graceland mansion in Memphis, Tennessee draws fans from all over the world, keen to pay their last respects to 'the King'. A tour of the 14-acre estate ends in the Meditation Garden where the tombs of Elvis and his family are sited.

COOKING TIPS

Re-roll the trimmings from the topping mixture and cut out tiny heart shapes or rounds. Arrange them in the gaps between the large scones • To peel the peaches easily, cut a slit in the skins and plunge the fruit into a bowl of hot water. Leave for 1 minute, then drain and peel off the skins.

SERVING TIP

For a summery meal, serve crab meat (fresh or tinned) with mayonnaise, potato salad and a green salad. If using fresh crab, arrange the meat in the empty shell to serve. Finish with the cobbler, drizzled with a little pouring cream.

SERVING TIP Serve this dessert after a hearty bowl of Jambalaya — rice cooked with tomatoes, peppers, celery and spicy seasonings, plus any combination of prawns, chicken, spicy sausage and smoked ham.

SPICED FRUITS WITH SABAYON

USA

INGREDIENTS

(Serves 4)

- 450g/1lb pears
- 225g/8oz cranberries
- ¼ tsp ground cloves
- ½ tsp ground ginger
- 100g/4oz caster sugar

FOR THE SABAYON

- 3 egg yolks
- 50g/2oz caster sugar
- 150ml/¼ pint dry white wine
- 15g/½oz cornflour

INGREDIENTS TIP

Use firm pears for this recipe so they hold their shape and texture when cooked. Over-ripe pears will be too soft.

Sabayon is a rich, frothy sauce served warm from the pan. Here it's spooned over chilled fruits spiced with ginger and cloves for a delicious hot and cold contrast.

1 Peel, core and slice the pears. Put into a saucepan with the cranberries, cloves, ginger, 100g/4oz sugar and 150ml/¼ pint of water. Bring to the boil, then cover and simmer for 10 minutes, or until the fruit is soft. Leave to cool, then chill for 1 hour, or until ready to serve.

Step 1

2 Just before serving, make the sabayon. Whisk the egg yolks and sugar in a large heatproof bowl until creamy. Gradually whisk in the wine.

Step 2

3 Set the bowl over a pan of gently simmering water. Whisk for 10 minutes, or until the mixture is frothy and thick. Add the cornflour and whisk in until the sauce is smooth and slightly thickened. Spoon the chilled fruit into serving dishes and spoon over the hot sabayon sauce. Serve.

Step 3

reparation: **20** Min Chilling: **1** Hour
ooking: **20** Min
er Serving: 263 kcal/1110 kJ;
g protein; 4g fat; 50g carbohydrate

TYPICALLY LOUISIANA

Much of the southern state of Louisiana is an unspoiled wilderness. Rolling hills covered with pine trees lead down to sub-tropical bayous. These lush swamp-like areas are awash with wildlife — from wading birds and pelicans to swamp rabbits and even alligators.

3 WAYS WITH CHOCOLATE AND BERRIES

Chocolate and strawberries make perfect partners. Try one of these recipes to enjoy this sweet combination at its best.

CHOCOLATE AND STRAWBERRY ROUNDS

Preparation: **40** Min, plus cooling Cooking: **25** Min

NORTHERN FRANCE

(SERVES 6)

- 175g/6oz soft-tub margarine
- 175g/6oz caster sugar
- 3 eggs
- 175g/6oz self-raising flour
- 1 tsp baking powder
- 25g/1oz cocoa
- 2 tbsp milk

FOR THE FILLING

- 2 tbsp brandy
- 225g/8oz strawberries
- 142ml/5fl oz double cream
- 100g/4oz fromage frais
- icing sugar, to dust

1 Preheat oven to 180°C/350°F/Gas 4. Line 27x19cm/11x7½in tin, or equivalent, with baking paper. Beat fat, sugar, eggs, flour, baking powder, cocoa and milk until smooth. Spoon into tin and spread level. Bake for 20–25 minutes, or until firm to touch. Turn out and cool.

2 Sprinkle the cake with brandy. Stamp out six 9cm/3½in rounds. Halve each round horizontally. Hull and slice the strawberries.

3 Whip cream to soft peaks and fold in fromage frais. Spread cream over brandy-soaked cakes. Add half the berries. Top with the remaining cake rounds. Arrange the remaining berries on top and dust with icing sugar.

CHOCOLATE AN

Preparation: **40** Min, plus cool

GREAT BRITAIN

(SERVES 6)

- 175g/6oz soft-tub margarine
- 175g/6oz caster sugar
- 3 eggs
- 175g/6oz self-raising flour
- 1 tsp baking powder
- 25g/1oz cocoa
- 2 tbsp milk

FOR THE FILLING

- 175g/6oz plain chocolate
- 4 tbsp strawberry jam
- 142ml/5fl oz double cream
- 6 strawberries

1 Preheat oven to 180°C/350°F/Gas 4. Line 18cm/7in square tin with baking paper. Beat fat,

Chocolate and Strawberry Trifle

Preparation: **40** Min, plus cooling Cooking: **25** Min

Great Britain

(SERVES 6)

- **100g/4oz soft-tub margarine**
- **100g/4oz caster sugar**
- **2 eggs, plus 3 egg yolks**
- **100g/4oz self-raising flour**
- **15g/½oz cocoa**
- **½ tsp baking powder**
- **3 tbsp milk**
- **4 tbsp strawberry jam**
- **350g/12oz strawberries**

FOR THE CUSTARD

- **100g/4oz plain chocolate**
- **300ml/½ pint milk**
- **284ml/10fl oz double cream**
- **50g/2oz caster sugar**
- **1 tbsp cornflour**

1 Preheat oven to 180°C/350°F/Gas 4. Line 15cm/6in square tin with baking paper. Beat the fat, sugar, 2 eggs, flour, cocoa, baking powder and 3 tablespoons milk until smooth. Spoon into tin. Bake for 25 minutes, or until firm. Cool.

2 For custard, heat chocolate, milk and half the cream in a pan. Whisk 3 yolks and 50g/2oz sugar until thick. Mix in cornflour. Whisk in chocolate cream. Cook gently, stirring, until thick. Cool.

3 Halve the cake, then sandwich with jam and cut into strips. Arrange strips in a bowl. Hull and halve the strawberries; add 225g/8oz to the bowl. Spoon custard over berries. Whip cream to soft peaks; swirl on top. Decorate with strawberries.

ꞏRAWBERRY BOXES

king: **40** Min

ıgar, eggs, flour, baking powder, ocoa and milk until smooth. poon into tin and spread level. ake for 35–40 minutes, or until rm. Turn out and cool.

2 Trim cake and slice top level. Cut into 6 equal squares. To ıake boxes, carefully hollow out ake, leaving a 1cm/½in border all ıe way round. Take care not to ıt through the base.

3 For filling, melt the chocolate. Brush over sides and top dges of cake boxes. Leave to set. poon 2 teaspoons of jam into ach box. Whip cream until stiff; ipe a rosette on top of the jam. op each one with a strawberry.

STRAWBERRIES WITH VANILLA CREAM

CHILE

INGREDIENTS

(Serves 4)

- 450g/1lb strawberries
- 3 tbsp caster sugar

FOR THE VANILLA CREAM

- 200ml/7fl oz double cream
- 1 egg
- 25g/1oz caster sugar
- ½ tsp vanilla essence
- 2–3 tbsp orange liqueur or orange juice
- 2 tbsp shelled pistachio nuts, to decorate

INGREDIENTS TIP

Pistachio nuts are a pretty pale green colour with red-purple skins. Use shelled, unsalted nuts for this dish.

A featherlight cream flavoured with vanilla and orange turns simple sliced strawberries into a gourmet treat. Chopped pistachio nuts add a colourful crunch.

1 Rinse and dry the strawberries, then hull and slice them. Put the slices in a bowl and sprinkle with 3 tablespoons of sugar. Cover with non-PVC cling film and chill in the fridge for 30 minutes.

Step 1

2 For the vanilla cream, whip the cream until stiff peaks form. In a separate large bowl, whisk the egg and sugar with an electric whisk until very thick and creamy. Gently fold in the whipped cream, vanilla essence and liqueur or orange juice.

Step 2

3 Roughly chop the pistachio nuts with a sharp knife. Layer the strawberries and vanilla cream in serving bowls. Sprinkle with the chopped nuts and serve immediately.

Step 3

Preparation: **20** Min Chilling: **30** Min
Per Serving: 425 kcal/1770 kJ;
5g protein; 30g fat; 34g carbohydrate

TYPICALLY CHILEAN

Santiago, the capital of Chile, is an amazing sight, surrounded by immense mountain peaks. The stylish Bellavista district is a popular meeting place for young people with its pretty tree-lined streets and smart pavement cafés and bars.

COOKING TIPS

Jse a large metal spoon or a spatula to fold the ream into the egg mixture, with a gentle cutting nd folding motion. This keeps as much air as possible n the mixture • For a special occasion, dip the rims f the dessert bowls in egg white then in caster sugar efore filling with the dessert to give a frosted effect.

SERVING TIP

Start the meal with a creamy avocado dip topped with crispy bacon strips. Serve cold prawns and tortilla chips for dipping. For a main course, serve grilled tuna steaks with a chilli and lime marinade and finish with the strawberry desserts.

Serving tip This refreshing dessert is perfect for cooling you down after a spicy beef chilli con carne served with sour cream and crisp tortilla chips or oven-baked potato wedges.

Frozen Strawberry Dessert

Mexico

INGREDIENTS

(Serves 4)

- 2 eggs
- 225g/8oz caster sugar
- 3 tsp vanilla sugar
- 200g/7oz natural yoghurt
- 225g/8oz strawberries
- ice cream wafers, to serve

Ingredients Tip

You can buy vanilla sugar (flavoured with synthetic vanilla) in large supermarkets but it is very easy to make your own. Bury a couple of vanilla pods in a jar of caster sugar and leave for 2 weeks for the flavours to infuse. If you don't have time, use plain caster sugar and add a few drops of vanilla essence.

This fruity frozen treat makes a light and refreshing dessert that's lower in fat than ice cream, and is much easier to make. It keeps for 3 months in the freezer so why not make double?

1 In a large bowl, whisk the eggs, caster and vanilla sugars with a balloon whisk until creamy. Stir in the yoghurt.

2 Wash the strawberries and pat dry. Hull them, then purée in a food processor or blender until smooth. Alternatively, push the berries through a fine sieve. Stir the purée into the yoghurt mixture.

3 Line a freezerproof container with non-PVC cling film, leaving some overhanging the edges. Spoon in the strawberry mixture. Freeze for 3½ hours, or until solid.

4 About 20 minutes before serving, transfer the dessert to the fridge. Scoop into four serving dishes and serve with wafer biscuits.

Step 1

Step 3

Step 4

Preparation: **10** Min
Freezing: 3½ Hours
Per Serving: 317 kcal/1345 kJ;
g protein; 3g fat; 70g carbohydrate

Typically Mexican

Ice creams, or *helados*, are a familiar treat throughout Mexico, but the best ones are believed to come from the Michoacán region. Flavoured with fresh fruits like strawberries, guava and mango, they are served in most cafés, or sold from road-side stalls.

RASPBERRY HEAVEN

SERBIA

INGREDIENTS

(Makes 4 desserts)

- 300ml/½ pint vanilla ice cream
- 250g/9oz raspberries
- 2 tbsp raspberry liqueur
- 32 small macaroon or ratafia biscuits
- 142ml/5fl oz double cream
- plain chocolate, to decorate

INGREDIENTS TIP

You can use frozen or tinned raspberries if fresh are not available. Drain off most of their juice, leaving about 2 tablespoons, before adding the liqueur.

The tangy raspberries, smooth ice cream, crunchy biscuits and rich dark chocolate in this simple dessert produce a flavour combination that will give your tastebuds a real treat.

1 Take the ice cream out of the freezer 20 minutes in advance to soften. Reserve a few raspberries for decoration and put the rest in a small pan with the liqueur. Heat gently for 5 minutes, or until the raspberries soften and juice starts to run from the fruit. Set aside to cool slightly.

Step 1

2 Crush 8 macaroon or ratafia biscuits. Sprinkle in the bottom of four dessert glasses. Cover with a few raspberries. Spoon the ice cream on top and press down lightly.

3 Break the remaining biscuits into pieces and add to the glasses. Spoon over the rest of the raspberries and their juice.

Step 3

4 Whip the cream until soft peaks form. Finely grate some plain chocolate. Add a dollop of cream to each dessert and sprinkle generously with grated chocolate.

Step 4

Preparation: **10** Min Cooking: **5** Min
Per Dessert: 556 kcal/2322 kJ;
8g protein; 34g fat; 55g carbohydrate

TYPICALLY SERBIAN

The beautiful five-domed monastery at Gracanica in Serbia was built in 1310 and is a fine example of Byzantine architecture. Different shades of sand and limestone give the outside its distinctive colour, while inside is a superb collection of frescoes.

COOKING TIPS

o crush the biscuits, put them in a plastic food ag and tap with a rolling pin until roughly crushed. Grate the chocolate on the fine side of a box grater r use a potato peeler to grate off fine shavings. It vill be easier to grate if you put the chocolate in he fridge for 20 minutes beforehand.

SERVING TIP

Brush aubergine slices and mushrooms with a little oil and cook on a griddle or in a large frying pan. Serve with slices of pastrami, cold beef or smoked salmon and some crusty farmhouse bread.

Serving tip For a Russian-style meal, start with blinis topped with sour cream and lumpfish roe, then serve beef stroganoff on a bed of rice. Finish with these berry desserts and a pot of strong coffee.

STRAWBERRY CHOUX PUFFS

RUSSIA

INGREDIENTS

(Makes 6 puffs)

- 75g/3oz butter
- 100g/4oz plain flour
- 3 eggs

FOR THE FILLING

- 225g/8oz strawberries
- 350g/12oz strawberry fromage frais
- 2 tsp icing sugar

INGREDIENTS TIP

Fromage frais is a fresh curd cheese made from skimmed cows' milk. It has a deceptively rich and velvety texture but is fairly low in fat.

For an elegant finale to a special meal, serve these luscious choux pastry rings. Surprisingly easy to make, just sandwich them together with creamy fromage frais and fill with berries.

1 Preheat the oven to 200°C/400°F/Gas 6. Put the butter in a pan with 200ml/7fl oz of water and bring to the boil. Sift the flour onto a sheet of greaseproof paper. When the water boils, remove from the heat and add the flour all at once. Beat well until the mixture forms a ball and leaves the sides of the pan clean. Cool slightly.

Step 1

2 Beat the eggs in a small bowl. Gradually add them to the pan, beating well between each addition, until the mixture is thick and glossy. Spoon into a piping bag fitted with a 1cm/½in star-shaped nozzle.

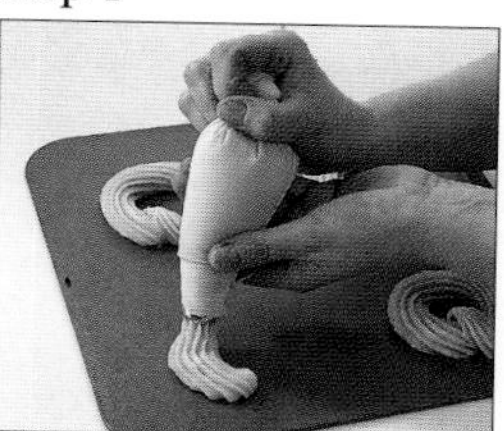

Step 3

3 Dampen 2 non-stick baking sheets. Pipe six rings, about 10cm/4in in diameter, onto the sheets. Bake for 25 minutes, or until golden brown and crisp. With a sharp knife, slice the rings in half while still hot. Leave to cool on a wire rack. Meanwhile, hull and quarter the strawberries.

Step 3

4 Put the bottom halves of the rings on serving plates. Spread with fromage frais and top with the remaining rings. Fill the centre of each ring with strawberries. Sift icing sugar over the top and serve.

Preparation: 40 Min
Cooking: 30 Min, plus cooling
Per Puff: 280 kcal/1170 kJ;
g protein; 17g fat; 25g carbohydrate

TYPICALLY RUSSIAN

The cathedral of St Basil the Blessed is sited at the southern end of Moscow's Red Square and is one of the most well known Russian buildings. The cathedral consists of eight churches and was built to commemorate Russia's victory over the Tartars in 1552.

*T*RADITIONAL GOOSEBERRY PIE

POLAND

INGREDIENTS

(Serves 6)

- 1 orange
- 500g/1lb 2oz shortcrust pastry
- 1 tsp ground ginger
- 1 egg yolk, to glaze

FOR THE FILLING

- 900g/2lb gooseberries
- 150g/5oz granulated sugar
- 1 tbsp cornflour
- 400g/14oz can red cherry pie filling

INGREDIENTS TIP

Fresh gooseberries are in season from May to August but you can often find frozen ones during the autumn and winter months. If using frozen berries, allow them to thaw completely before using.

Filled with gooseberries and gooey cherries, this old-fashioned fruit pie is best served warm. The sweet ginger and orange pastry adds an extra treat to this family pudding.

1 Preheat oven to 220°C/425°F/Gas 7. Grate the rind from the orange. On a floured surface, roll out half the pastry to a 30cm/12in round. Sprinkle over half the ginger and orange rind and lightly roll in. Use the pastry to line a 23cm/9in flan or pie dish. Chill.

Step 1

2 For the filling, wash, top and tail the gooseberries. Put the sugar and cornflour into a bowl. Stir in the gooseberries and cherry pie filling. Spoon into the pastry case and sprinkle over 2 tablespoons of water.

3 Roll out the remaining pastry to a 30cm/12in round, reserving the trimmings for decoration. Sprinkle over the remaining ginger and orange rind and roll in. Lay the pastry over the filling and press to seal. Flute the pastry edge with your fingers.

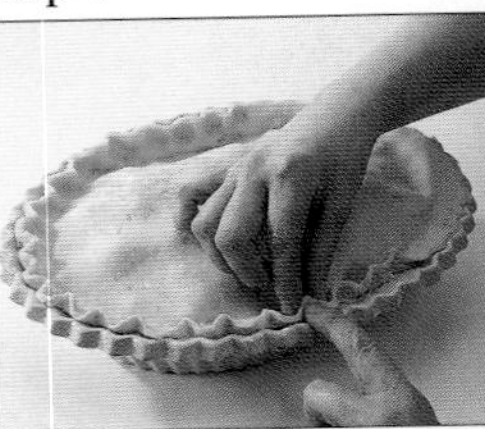

Step 3

4 Beat the egg yolk with 1 tablespoon of water and brush over the pastry. Re-roll the trimmings and cut out leaf shapes. Stick the leaves on the pie with the egg glaze and brush all over. Cut 3 steam holes in the lid. Bake for 10 minutes. Reduce the oven heat to 190°C/375°F/Gas 5. Bake for a further 25 minutes, or until golden brown. Serve warm.

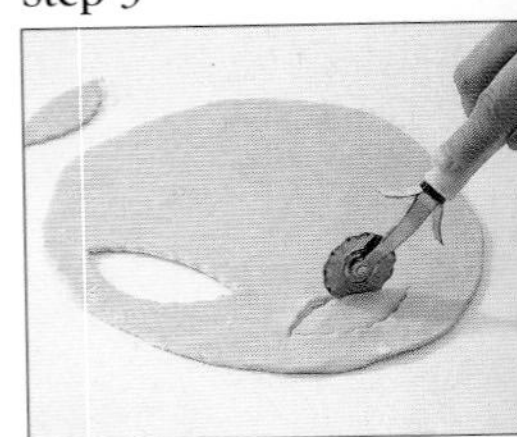

Step 4

Preparation: 30 Min Cooking: 35 Min
Per Serving: 583 kcal/2444 kJ;
7g protein; 25g fat; 88g carbohydrate

TYPICALLY POLISH

The Palace of Culture and Science is one of the most striking buildings in Warsaw. Originally a gift from the Soviet Union and named after Joseph Stalin, it is now the city's cultural centre, containing two theatres, three cinemas and two museums.

COOKING TIPS

he gooseberries need to be topped and tailed before sing. Wash the berries and pat dry, then use a pair of harp kitchen scissors to trim both ends • Adding ornflour to the filling stops the juices from the ooseberries making the pastry soggy.

SERVING TIP

Start the meal with sausages served with hot sauerkraut or baked potatoes and a dollop of mustard. Follow with the warm pie and a generous spoonful of custard or cream.

DICTIONARY OF TERMS

A guide to some of the flavourings and ingredients used in this book, plus hints on using eggs, and what sort of cream is best for whipping, pouring and boiling.

Choux Pastry is different to other pastries as it is cooked twice. During baking, the eggs make the pastry puff up into crisp, light airy shells that are then split and filled to make buns, éclairs and profiteroles.

Cinnamon is made from the dried bark of a tropical evergreen tree. It is sold in small brown sticks or ground to powder form. The sticks are good for infusing custards, sauces and poached or stewed fruit, while the ground version is ideal for cakes and puddings. The warm flavour goes especially well with chocolate, apples and coffee.

Clear or Runny Honey is better for cooking than the set variety as it blends easily and dissolves quickly. It is good in mousses, jellies, ice creams and other creamy desserts. It also makes an excellent sweetener for stewed fruit and fruit salads instead of ordinary sugar.

EGG SAFETY

Some of the recipes in this book contain eggs that are raw or lightly cooked (*pages 8/9, 10/11, 16/17, 28/29, 48/49, 52/53, 54/55*). To avoid the risk of salmonella poisoning, these dishes should not be eaten by infants, pregnant women, the elderly or anyone who is ill. Here are some egg safety tips and a guide to using substitutes.

EGG TIPS

- *Always use eggs within their 'best before' date and put them in the fridge as soon as possible after buying.*
- *Check for the Lion Mark which ensures that hygienic production standards have been used.*
- *Bacteria can enter an egg through cracks in the shell, so only buy eggs with clean, undamaged shells.*
- *Use foods containing raw eggs within 2 days.*

EGG SUBSTITUTES

Powdered egg and powdered egg white are pasteurized so are safe to use in desserts for the 'at risk' groups listed above. They are available from most large supermarkets. Follow the instructions on the packet for reconstituting with water then use as directed in the recipe.

Cornflour is ground from maize kernels and is used as a thickening agent for sweet and savoury sauces. Some cakes and biscuits can also be made with cornflour.

Gelatine is a setting agent that comes in either leaf or powdered form. Both leaf and powdered are interchangeable in the recipes — use 1 sachet of powdered gelatine or 4 sheets of leaf to set 600ml/1 pint of mixture. (See pages 4/5 for how to use them.) A vegetarian substitute is also available from most supermarkets but check the packet instructions as strengths of setting may vary.

Liqueurs can be flavoured with fruit, herbs, seeds or nuts. Most soft fruits and berries are used in many different liqueurs, such as blackcurrants (crème de cassis), raspberries (crème de framboise) and cherries (cherry brandy). Liqueurs can be used to flavour sweet creams, custards and ice creams, soaked into cakes, or stirred into fruit salads, crumbles or pie fillings. Alternatively, serve them in small glasses with dessert, or add a dash to the after-dinner coffees.

Nutmeg is available whole or ground and has a warm, sweet, nutty flavour. It is used in cakes, biscuits, milk puddings and custards as well as pasta, sauces and potato dishes. It also goes well with pumpkin, cheese and spinach. It is best used freshly grated as the aromatic flavour starts to deteriorate once it is ground. Small graters, especially for nutmeg, are available from department stores and bookshops.

Passion-fruit originally came from Brazil but are now grown in Kenya and South America too. They are small oval fruit with reddish-purple wrinkled skin. Inside are small edible black seeds set in fragrant green-orange pulp. Just cut the fruit in half and scoop out the seeds and pulp with a spoon (both are edible). The intense, sweet flavour of the passion-fruit is delicious in fruit salads, ice creams and sorbets, or spooned over creamy desserts.

Pecan Nuts come from the USA and are part of the hickory family. The nuts are enclosed in smooth olive-shaped shells. The kernel inside is in two halves and looks similar to a walnut. The sweet rich flavour makes the nuts a favourite in sugary desserts, especially the classic American sweet, pecan pie.

Types of Cream

A quick guide to the different types of cream and their uses.

Creme fraiche
Has a fat content of 35–60% and a faintly tangy flavour. Good for cooking as it does not separate.

Double cream
Ideal for pouring, whipping and piping. It has a fat content of 48% so it can be boiled. If whipping, take care not to overbeat. Can be frozen.

Single cream
Has a fat content of 18% so should not be boiled or it will curdle. Perfect for pouring and for enriching sauces. Not suitable for freezing.

Sour cream
Has a fat content of 21% and a spoonable consistency. It can be heated but is not good at very high temperatures. Often used for cold dips and sauces. Not suitable for freezing.

Whipping cream
Has a fat content of about 35% and is good for whipping and piping. For best results, make sure the cream, bowl and whisk are cold before whipping. It can be frozen successfully.

Puff Pastry is light, flaky and buttery and is used to make a variety of sweet and savoury creations, such as croissants, vols-au-vents, tarts and palmier biscuits. It is also used as a wrapping for fruits, cheese or meat. Making puff pastry is a complex procedure involving rolling, folding and turning the dough six times, and chilling it between each turn. To save you the time and effort, good quality ready-made puff pastry is sold in most supermarkets, either as a block or a ready-rolled strip.

Sabayon is a classic French sauce made from egg yolks, sugar and wine whisked over a gentle heat until thick, frothy and creamy. As well as pouring it over soft fruits as a sauce, try serving it with warm fruit compôte and poached fruit, pour it over hot fruit tarts, or spoon around individual sponge puddings instead of the traditional custard.

INDEX

Acknowledgments

Picture Credits
All cover and recipe pictures
Meister Verlag/International Masters Publishers B.V.
Some by Philip Wilkins
Agency pictures for 'Typically' sections
AllOver: Kröner, page 19; Mark Azavedo: David Foreman, page 52; Bilderberg: Blickle, page 6; Britstock-IFA: page 60; Hans Strand, page 16; Spencer Grant, page 20; Günter Graefenhain, page 25; Lecom, page 33; Gottschalk, page 40; Corbis: Otto Lang, page 56; Nik Wheeler, page 37; Fahn, page 30; Robert Harding: page 14; Schuster, page 22; S Knophius, page 59; Look: Heeb, page 26; Mauritius: Rossenbach, page 9; Raga, page 34; David Noble, pages 10, 13, 44, 49; Schapowalow: Comnet, page 43; Hilmer, page 55; Travel Ink: Mathieu Lamarre, page 38; Ronald Badkin, page 46;

Recipes containing raw egg should not be eaten by infants, pregnant women, the elderly or those who are ill. Eggs are medium unless stated. Teaspoons and tablespoons are level and measured using standard measuring spoons. Follow either metric or imperial measurements and don't mix the two.

Reproduced by Mullis Morgan, London, UK
Printed in Verona, Italy by Mondadori